Reading Comprehension

Written by Trisha Callella

Editor: Denise Skomer

Illustrator: Catherine Rader

Cover Illustrator: Tim Huhn

Designer: Terri Lamadrid

Cover Designer: Barbara Peterson

Art Director: Tom Cochrane

Project Director: Carolea Williams

Table of Contents

Introduction

Learning to read is a magical and mysterious journey in a child's life. Letters that one day appear as strange, unrecognizable symbols, suddenly become a code for unlocking secret messages and hidden adventures. Of course, learning to read means more than simply decoding. It means comprehending the message woven within the text.

Reading Comprehension is designed to help you guide students toward becoming better readers. This book addresses eleven strategies necessary for developing effective comprehension skills. Teach students techniques for monitoring their comprehension, and give them a variety of tools to self-correct mistakes while reading. Combine modeling of skills with direct instruction to present information in a meaningful, easy-to-understand manner.

As students begin to move beyond mere decoding to a greater understanding of text, they see that print contains a message to be remembered, elaborated on, and connected in a meaningful way with their daily life. *Reading Comprehension* provides a plan of action for moving beyond assessment to instruction through the use of skill-building activities that incorporate key comprehension strategies.

Keep *Reading Comprehension* close at hand throughout the school year. You will find a wealth of information and ideas to turn your beginning readers into proficient readers who successfully comprehend text. The better and more efficiently students read, the more successful they will be in school. More importantly, students will develop a love of reading and a desire to become lifelong learners.

What we become depends on what we read after all the professors have finished with us. The greatest university of all is a collection of books.
—Thomas Carlyle

Strategic Readers

Using the right tool makes a job easier. Like a master carpenter, a master reader needs to have a wealth of tools available to make the job of comprehending text more efficient. Students need to become strategic readers because reading is a core component of almost every other lesson they will learn in school and in life. Early reading success is a predictor of later academic success. With so much research pointing toward the benefits of teaching students to become successful readers, instructing them in how to read strategically is a logical plan of action.

What are the characteristics of strategic readers? For the purposes of this book, strategic readers are defined as students who

- identify difficult words in the text and know several ways to determine their meaning
- read fluently in phrases or sections so as to comprehend the meaning of the text
- see the order of events in sequence and understand how sequential elements build to tell a story
- can summarize and organize the elements of a story in a retelling
- make predictions about what will happen next in the text
- have the ability to access prior knowledge about a subject in order to focus on the text and make logical predictions
- identify the characters in a story and show an understanding of each character's role
- have the ability to categorize events and ideas from a story into groups based on how they are similar
- can identify and communicate the main idea of a piece of text
- move beyond the literal level of the text by making inferences and elaborating on known details
- connect what they read with other books, with their own lives, and with the world around them

Assessing Students' Needs

Before planning your reading instruction, take the time to assess the reading strategies of each student in your class. The following ideas will guide you in determining base-level information about each student. Use this information to individualize instruction and for formal and informal assessments to gauge student growth throughout the year.

- Use the assessment questions on pages 6–7 to determine if a student needs further development in any of the eleven strategies of reading comprehension. If the answer is "yes" to one or more of the questions in a particular strategy, make a note that the student needs instruction in that skill. Plan whole-class, small-group, or individual lessons as needed for each skill.

- Take time to read one-on-one with each student. Pull students from center groups, or meet with individuals during writing or silent-reading time. Ask students to read short stories or selected passages from age-appropriate materials, or invite them to read aloud from their independent-reading book. Ask students questions before, during, and after reading to determine their understanding. Make anecdotal notes after each reading session, and include them in students' assessment portfolios (see page 8).

- Use prepared assessment instruments that correlate with your reading program. Combine information gained from these tests with the notes you gather from observations of each student.

- Record anecdotal information about individual students on sticky notes as you observe them reading independently, working in reading groups, or reading in other curricular areas. Place the sticky notes on a clipboard, and at a break or at the end of the day, transfer this data into students' assessment portfolios.

- Write each student's name on a separate index card. Hole-punch the top left corner of each card. Arrange the cards alphabetically by last name on a large notebook ring or a shower curtain ring. Hang the ring from one of your belt loops, or attach it to your plan book. Write observations of each student as you walk around the classroom, or use the index cards to record the results of informal assessments. When you fill an index card, place it in the student's assessment portfolio, and replace it with a new card.

Assessment Questions

Use the following questions to determine if your students need additional instruction in any of the reading strategies outlined in this book. Keep these questions in mind as you work with all your students, or use them to develop a formal assessment tool for those students with the most need. If a student needs additional instruction in a particular area, refer to the pages listed after each strategy to find related activities.

Word-Attack Skills (see pp. 9–15)
Does the student . . .
- stop at unfamiliar words and become frustrated?
- skip over difficult or unfamiliar words and not look back?
- ignore picture cues or surrounding words when faced with new words?

Phrasing and Fluency (see pp. 16–22)
Does the student . . .
- read each word individually?
- become focused on decoding each word and ignore punctuation marks?
- sound choppy when reading aloud?

Sequencing (see pp. 23–31)
Does the student . . .
- have difficulty with labeling and identifying simple patterns using manipulatives?
- find it confusing when asked to physically order objects in a given sequence?
- become confused by the order in which events take place in a story?

Retelling (see pp. 32–37)
Does the student . . .
- have difficulty remembering the key elements in a story?
- become frustrated when asked to tell a story in his or her own words?
- retell a story in a jumbled manner, making it difficult to follow?

Predicting (see pp. 38–44)
Does the student . . .
- repeat answers given by others when asked to make predictions?
- express apprehension either verbally or physically when asked to make predictions?
- make random guesses that are unrelated to the story?

Accessing Prior Knowledge (see pp. 45–52)
Does the student . . .
- find it difficult to relate story events to his or her own life?
- avoid contributing to discussions where students share experiences?
- have limited experiences from which to draw?

Characterization (see pp. 53–57)

Does the student . . .

- have difficulty describing characters beyond physical attributes and actions?
- find it difficult to remember the characters in the story?
- often confuse characters?

Categorization (see pp. 58–65)

Does the student . . .

- have difficulty sorting items by similar attributes?
- find it difficult to pick out specific details in a story?
- have trouble identifying story elements?

Identifying the Main Idea (see pp. 66–72)

Does the student . . .

- find it difficult to rephrase things he or she hears?
- verbally summarize what he or she reads?
- have difficulty answering the question *What was the story about?*

Making Inferences (see pp. 73–79)

Does the student . . .

- focus only on literal details?
- have trouble answering how and why questions?
- understand cause and effect?

Making Connections (see pp. 80–93)

Does the student . . .

- find it difficult relating what is read to his or her own life?
- have trouble relating people, places, and things from stories to what he or she knows?
- have difficulty seeing how two or more books are related?

Managing Information

Keeping track of your assessment data can be cumbersome and confusing unless you develop a clear organizational plan. The following suggestions provide ideas for keeping your assessment data conveniently at hand:

- Write each student's name on a separate file folder. Place assessment data and anecdotal information into the folder for easy access, and store the folders in a plastic storage crate. Place in the folder the sticky notes and index cards you accumulate as you informally assess student performance.
- Write each student's name on a separate index card. Record the skills that each student needs to work on, and refer to the cards when you plan small-group or one-on-one lessons. As a student masters each of the skills on the card, highlight the skill, and write the date. Refer to the cards when preparing for parent/teacher conferences or when completing report cards.
- Maintain oral records of each student's reading ability by tape-recording read-aloud sessions. Label a tape for each student, and store the tapes in student assessment portfolios. Periodically ask each student to read a selected passage, and conduct an informal question-and-answer session to assess comprehension. By the end of the year, you will have individual progress records to share with students and parents.

Designing Instruction

Use the information from your formal and informal assessments to plan your reading instruction. Here are a few ways to organize instruction using this data:

- Pull assessment information for an individual student, and work one-on-one with that student to teach a specific strategy.
- Teach mini-lessons to small groups of students who need reinforcement on a particular skill. Change groups regularly based on developmental needs. Pull students for mini-lessons during center time, silent-reading time, or independent-writing time.
- Build whole-class lessons around a particular reading strategy. Use an overhead projector and transparencies to present examples of text, and model each skill. Devote a lesson each week to a particular skill, and regularly review previously taught skills.

Use parent volunteers and classroom assistants to work with small groups or individual students. Provide materials and simple training to volunteers, and assign specific blocks of time for them to work with students. Use this time as an opportunity to work with other students or complete follow-up assessment to determine student growth.

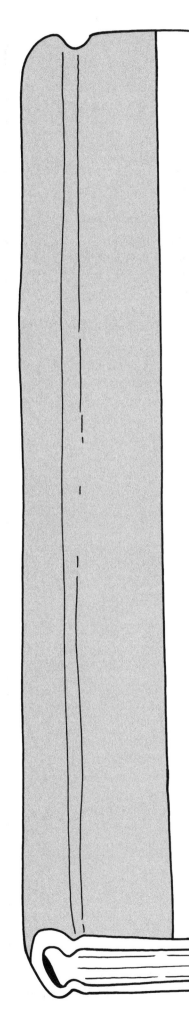

Word-Attack Skills

What Is the Skill?

Unfamiliar words are a roadblock to understanding the meaning of text. The first step in becoming a strategic reader is figuring out ways to decode and define new words.

Why Do Students Need to Know It?

In order for students to comprehend what they read, they must first have the ability to decode unfamiliar words and determine their meaning. Students must monitor their reading to make sure that the words make sense, sound right, and look right. The key is for students to have a variety of strategies at their fingertips that they can internalize and use independently when they encounter new or difficult words.

Teaching Tips

Be sure that students are reading material at their instructional level. When students encounter a great number of difficult words, they tend to become frustrated. Give them material that is challenging, but not overwhelming. Create many opportunities to model "word-attack skills" for students. These examples will make the skills more concrete and easier for students to understand. In this section, you will find resources to help students identify unfamiliar words and monitor their own reading.

Word-Attack Bookmark

Materials
- Word-Attack Bookmark (page 11)
- chart paper
- scissors
- crayons or markers

In advance, make a class set of the Word-Attack Bookmark, and copy each word-attack tool from the bookmark onto a piece of chart paper. Cut out the bookmarks. Give each student a bookmark to decorate. Then, use the information at the bottom of this page to introduce each word-attack tool and explain how the tool is used during reading. Provide examples to help students understand each strategy. After reviewing the tools on the list, ask students to share any additional strategies they use to figure out unfamiliar words. If a student repeats a strategy already on the list, acknowledge his or her response by rephrasing it to match the list. For example, say *Yes, John, using the letters in the word to figure out how it sounds would be like sound out the word.* If a new strategy is given, add it to the chart paper, and have students write it on their bookmark. Invite students to use the bookmark in their independent reading. Remind them to refer to the word-attack strategies when they come across new or unfamiliar words.

Reread the sentence.
Remind students to reread the sentence more than once and think about what word might make sense.

Sound out the word.
Show students how to blend the sounds of the word together and try to pronounce it.

Use picture clues.
Encourage students to review the pictures on the page and see if they provide any clues to help them figure out the unfamiliar word.

Look for chunks in the word.
Have students look for letter chunks in the word that might be familiar. Invite students to read each chunk separately and then blend the chunks together to sound out the entire word (e.g., unknown word: *fantastic*, chunks: *fan- tas- tic*).

Connect to a word you know.
Tell students to think of a word that looks like the unknown word. Have them compare the two words and use the known word to figure out the meaning of the unfamiliar word (e.g., unknown word: *judgement*, known word: *judge*).

Read on to look for clues.
Tell students that when they reach an unfamiliar word they should read on a bit and try to think about what might make sense. Then, have students go back and reread the sentence with the word they think makes the most sense.

Word-Attack Bookmark

Reread the sentence.

Sound out the word.

Use picture clues.

Look for chunks in the word.

Connect to a word you know.

Read on to look for clues.

_____

_____

_____

Name _____

Reread the sentence.

Sound out the word.

Use picture clues.

Look for chunks in the word.

Connect to a word you know.

Read on to look for clues.

_____

_____

_____

Name _____

Name That Tool

Materials

- The Surprise reproducible (page 13)
- Word-Attack Bookmark (page 11)
- overhead transparency/projector

Make an overhead transparency of The Surprise reproducible, and introduce or review the strategies on the Word-Attack Bookmark. Have students listen and follow along as you read aloud the story from the transparency. Select one of the word-attack strategies from the bookmark, and model how to use it to figure out the first underlined word. Verbalize your thought process as shown below in the first example. Then, select a student to identify the word-attack tool you modeled. Ask the student to explain how he or she figured out which tool you used. Continue reading the passage, and model a different word-attack tool with each underlined word. Occasionally make a mistake in your modeling. This will help students to understand how to fix errors, especially those that affect the meaning of the story. (The second example shows an error being made and corrected.)

- You reach the word *strange* in the story and you stop.
- Say *I'm at a word I don't know. I'll reread the sentence to see what would make sense.*
- Reread and stop. Say *It could be* loud, *but that begins with a /l/. Let me read it again and get my mouth ready with the first sound /st/.*
- Reread again. *The students heard a /st/ . . . sound outside their classroom door.*
- Sound out the word, and reread the sentence using the correct word.
- Say *Let me sound out the rest of the word. The students heard a <u>strange</u> sound outside their classroom door. That makes sense in this sentence. I think I'll read on now.*

- You reach the word *books* in the story.
- Say *I'm at a word I don't know. I'll sound out the word and see if it makes sense. I see a /b/ sound and an /o/ sound and a /k/ sound. I think the word is* box.
- Reread the sentence using the new word. *It was filled with new box. That doesn't seem to make sense. Let me look at the word. It looks like* looks—*a word I know. It begins with a /b/ sound though. Let me try the word* books.
- Reread again. *It was filled with <u>books</u>. Now that makes sense!*

The Surprise

Reading time was almost over when the students heard a <u>strange</u> sound outside their classroom door. When the teacher opened the door, the students were <u>shocked</u> to find a huge package <u>wrapped</u> in blue paper. There was a note attached that read, *This is for the super students in this room!*

Everyone gathered around the <u>mysterious</u> package. "Who do you think left this present for us?" asked one student.

"I don't know," said the teacher. "Let's open it and see what is inside. Maybe then we will have a <u>clue</u> about who could have left it for us."

The students helped the teacher open the package. What a surprise! It was filled with new <u>books</u>. There was another note inside. This one read,

Dear class,
I came by to peek in your room, and I saw great reading.
You deserve this surprise. Enjoy! Happy Reading!
From,
The Principal

The students were <u>thrilled</u> to have new books for their classroom. They decided to write thank-you notes to the principal. They wrapped the notes inside a box and left it outside the principal's door. They hoped the principal would be as surprised as they were.

13

My Strategy Chart

Materials
- My Strategies Chart (page 15)
- Word-Attack Bookmark (page 11)

In advance, give each student a copy of the My Strategies Chart, and then introduce or review the strategies on the Word-Attack Bookmark. Have students monitor their independent reading for one week and use the strategies on the bookmark to help them identify unfamiliar words. Have students make a tally mark in the corresponding column of their strategy chart each time they use one of the strategies. If they use more than one tool for a particular word, have them mark all tools that apply. Ask students to store the chart in a reading folder.

At the end of the week, collect and review the charts. Schedule a short reading conference with each student to review his or her chart. Discuss the strategies each student used, and have the student demonstrate a few of the strategies during the conference. Use the information you learn to individualize each student's reading instruction. Provide mini-lessons on strategies that students seem to use infrequently or those they appear to not fully understand. Make suggestions for future use of the tools in each student's independent reading. After each conference, write the date at the top the chart, and place it in the student's reading folder. Have each student continue monitoring his or her use of word-attack strategies on a new copy of the chart. Periodically conference with students and make notes about their progress. Use the charts as a resource during parent/teacher conferences, and refer to them when completing progress reports.

My Strategies Chart

Name _____   Date _____

Directions: Make a tally mark next to each tool you use to figure out unfamiliar words.

Strategies	Number of Times Used
I reread the sentence.	
I sounded out the word.	
I used the picture clues.	
I looked for chunks in the word.	
I made a connection to another word that looked like the unfamiliar word.	
I read on to look for clues and then went back to the unfamiliar word.	

Reading Comprehension © 2000 Creative Teaching Press

Phrasing and Fluency

What Is the Skill?

Phrasing is reading in phrases or sections, a few words at a time. It is sometimes referred to as "reading like we are talking" because the words flow smoothly together. The message is easily understood because the words connect in a meaningful way. The focus is not on each individual word, but rather on a string of words that forms a complete thought.

Why Do Students Need to Know It?

Students who do not read with phrasing are usually "voice pointing," or reading words individually with their voice. The sound is robotic and interferes with their ability to comprehend the meaning of the text. Students need to learn to use phrasing in order to move beyond the decoding of individual words. Phrasing allows students to begin to connect individual words within a sentence and to see that the words relate to create meaning. Phrasing also builds fluency, which makes reading more productive and efficient for students.

Teaching Tips

Book selection is very important when teaching phrasing. The book must have natural language. If it is stilted, contrived, or incomplete in sentence structure, then students will not be able to effectively practice or understand the concept of fluency. Try to incorporate phrasing practice into all types of reading. Model phrasing during your read-aloud time, practice during shared- and guided-reading activities, and remind students to use phrasing during their independent reading. Finally, make sure students select books that are at their instructional level. The focus for phrasing should be on reading for fluency. If students are reading material above their level, they will get stuck on decoding unfamiliar words and will not be able to attend to phrasing. Poetry books are highly effective tools to use in teaching phrasing.

Phrasing Practice

Materials

- At the Farm reproducible (page 18)
- At the Movies reproducible (page 19)
- A Ride in Space reproducible (page 20)
- overhead transparencies/ projector
- favorite classroom book

Make overhead transparencies of the At the Farm, At the Movies, and A Ride in Space reproducibles. Use the At the Farm story set for the first lesson. In advance, fill in the blanks in the story with the names of your students or teachers from your school. Students will enjoy the familiarity.

Begin the lesson by demonstrating to students why phrasing is important. Select a book, and read aloud a few sentences. Do not use phrasing when you read. Instead, pause after every word to accentuate the delay. Have student volunteers comment on the way you are reading and explain why it is hard to understand. Then, introduce the concept of phrasing. Tell them that phrasing involves reading groups of words together. Explain that phrasing is reading like we talk and that grouping words in this way helps you better understand the meaning of what you read.

Place the At the Farm transparency on an overhead projector. Cover the transparency with a plain sheet of paper. Uncover one phrase at a time. Read each phrase aloud, have students read it with you, and then have them read the phrase without your assistance. Follow this procedure for each phrase in the story. At the end of the passage, reread the whole story as a class, using the phrases. Next, reveal the story, written as a paragraph, at the bottom of the reproducible. Have the class read aloud the text together, and then ask for volunteers to read it alone. End the lesson by having students verbalize why phrasing is an important part of reading. Encourage them to try phrasing when they read independently.

Use the At the Movies and A Ride in Space reproducibles to provide students with further phrasing practice, or create your own phrasing guides with text from your reading program or an age-appropriate book.

At the Farm

_____ and _____

went to the farm.

They saw

two dirty pigs,

four fuzzy chicks,

six little ducks,

eight red roosters,

and ten funny goats.

They had a great time.

At the Farm

_____ and _____ went to the

farm. They saw two dirty pigs, four fuzzy chicks, six little ducks, eight red

roosters, and ten funny goats. They had a great time.

Reading Comprehension © 2000 Creative Teaching Press

At the Movies

_____, _____, and _____

went to see

a movie together.

They were hungry,

so they bought

a tub of popcorn,

two cups of soda,

a pack of licorice,

and a chocolate bar.

Then they went in

to watch the movie.

At the Movies

_____, _____, and _____

went to see a movie together. They were hungry, so they bought a tub of

popcorn, two cups of soda, a pack of licorice, and a chocolate bar. Then

they went in to watch the movie.

A Ride in Space

_____, _____, and _____

went for a ride

on a spaceship.

They went to see

the Moon.

On their way,

they saw

some stars,

a comet,

and the planet Earth.

It was exciting!

A Ride in Space

_____, _____, and

_____ went for a ride on a spaceship. They went

to see the Moon. On their way, they saw some stars, a comet, and the

planet Earth. It was exciting!

Reading Comprehension © 2000 Creative Teaching Press

Pocket Chart Phrasing

Materials
- sentence strips
- pocket chart

Write each row of text shown below on a separate sentence strip. Place the sentence strips, in the order they are given, into a pocket chart so that the phrases are in successive rows. Read aloud the strips, one at a time, and have the class repeat each phrase aloud after you. Continue to the end of the story. Next, have the class reread the story in phrases without you. Finally, ask students to whisper the story quietly to themselves so they can gain independent practice without the pressure of reading alone in front of their classmates.

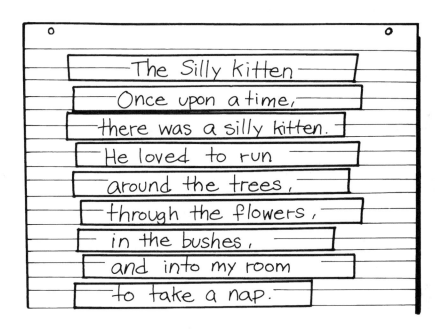

The Silly kitten
Once upon a time,
there was a silly kitten.
He loved to run
around the trees,
through the flowers,
in the bushes,
and into my room
to take a nap.

Independent Phrasing

Materials
- The Picnic reproducible (page 22)

Give each student a copy of The Picnic reproducible. Read aloud the story to familiarize the class with the language. Ask students to rewrite the story on the blank lines, breaking it into phrases. Have students write one phrase on each line. Then, pair each student with a partner, and ask the pairs to read their stories to each other, using the phrasing they chose. Follow up with a class discussion, and comment on the different ways students found to phrase the paragraph. Be sure to mention that there is more than one correct way to complete this task.

The Picnic

Name _____   Date _____

Directions: Rewrite this story using phrasing.

Our family went on a picnic. My mother packed our lunch. She brought some bread, a jar of peanut butter, a jar of jelly, some pickles, and a box of cookies. We ate and played all afternoon.

_____

_____

_____

_____

_____

_____

_____

_____

_____

Reading Comprehension © 2000 Creative Teaching Press

Sequencing

What Is the Skill?

Sequencing is the ability to put objects, activities, and events in a logical order. It involves being able to see the big picture of the story as opposed to focusing on the individual details.

Why Do Students Need to Know It?

Sequencing is an important part of understanding the message in the text. Events in a story build upon each other, moving from a beginning to an end in a logical order. Seeing this pattern will enable students to gain a more sophisticated understanding of what they read.

Teaching Tips

Sequencing involves several stages of development. Begin instruction at the most simple level, and progress toward a more difficult level as students find success. The activities in this section follow a progression of development as shown below:

1. order objects in a given sequence
2. order the steps in a familiar hands-on activity
3. order pictures that tell a story
4. order sentences of a story into a beginning, a middle, and an end

Object Ordering

Materials

- scissors
- plastic drinking straws
- overhead projector
- yarn
- construction paper
- glue

In advance, cut five plastic drinking straws to different lengths. Then, cut five different-sized pieces of yarn for each student. Place the straws on an overhead projector. Ask students to help you put the straws in order from shortest to longest. Have students verbalize how they knew where to place each straw. Give each student a set of yarn pieces. Have students put their yarn in order from shortest to longest. Assist those who are having difficulty, and check all student work for accuracy. Have students glue their yarn pieces on construction paper and share their results with a classmate.

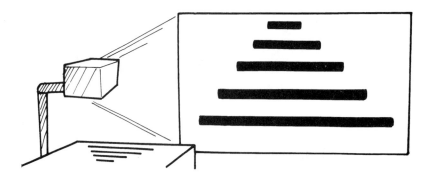

Partner Pantomime

Materials

- scrap paper
- container
- paper

In advance, write on separate pieces of scrap paper several activities that would be familiar to students (e.g., brushing your teeth, taking a bath, riding a bike). Place the scraps of paper in a container. Pair each student with a partner. Have each pair select one paper from the container. Give partners 5–10 minutes to write down all the steps involved in completing their activity. Then, have the pairs practice pantomiming the steps. Bring the class back together, and invite pairs to take turns acting out the steps of their activity in the correct sequence. Have the class guess what action each pair pantomimed.

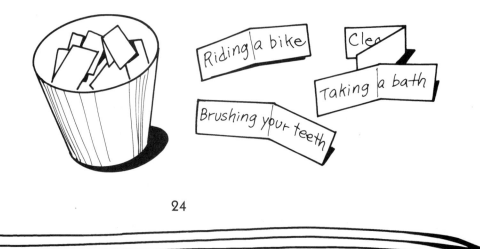

Picture-Perfect

Materials
- Picture-Perfect reproducible (page 26)
- scissors
- glue
- construction paper
- crayons or markers

Give each student a copy of the Picture-Perfect reproducible. Ask students to identify what each picture represents, and explain that the pictures show a series of events from a story. Have students cut out each picture and arrange the events in the correct sequence on their desk. Check each student's order for accuracy, and assist those who are having difficulty. Then, ask students to glue their pictures on a piece of construction paper in the correct order. Invite students to color the pictures when they are finished. Display the picture stories for all to enjoy.

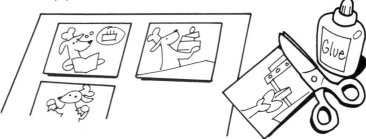

Get on Board

Materials
- Get on Board reproducibles (pages 27–29)
- scissors
- glue
- construction paper (assorted colors)
- tape
- butcher paper
- simple story
- chart paper

In advance, make a copy of the Get on Board reproducibles. Cut out the train cars, and glue each cutout to a different-colored piece of construction paper. Write *Beginning* in the center of the train engine, *Middle* in the center of the freight car, and *Ending* in the center of the caboose. Laminate the cars for durability, and tape them on a wall or board in three columns. Hang a long piece of butcher paper under each car. Select a simple story, or write one of your own. (Be sure the story has an obvious beginning, middle, and end.) Try to limit the story to five to seven sentences. Write the story on a piece of chart paper, and display it. Read aloud the story. Then, invite students to assist you in identifying each sentence as part of the beginning, middle, or end of the story. Write the sentences for each part of the story in the corresponding column on the butcher paper. Then, read the story together, and point to each sentence as students read. Leave the story on display for students to refer to as they work on sequencing.

Picture-Perfect

Directions: Cut out each picture. Put the pictures in the correct order.

Reading Comprehension © 2000 Creative Teaching Press

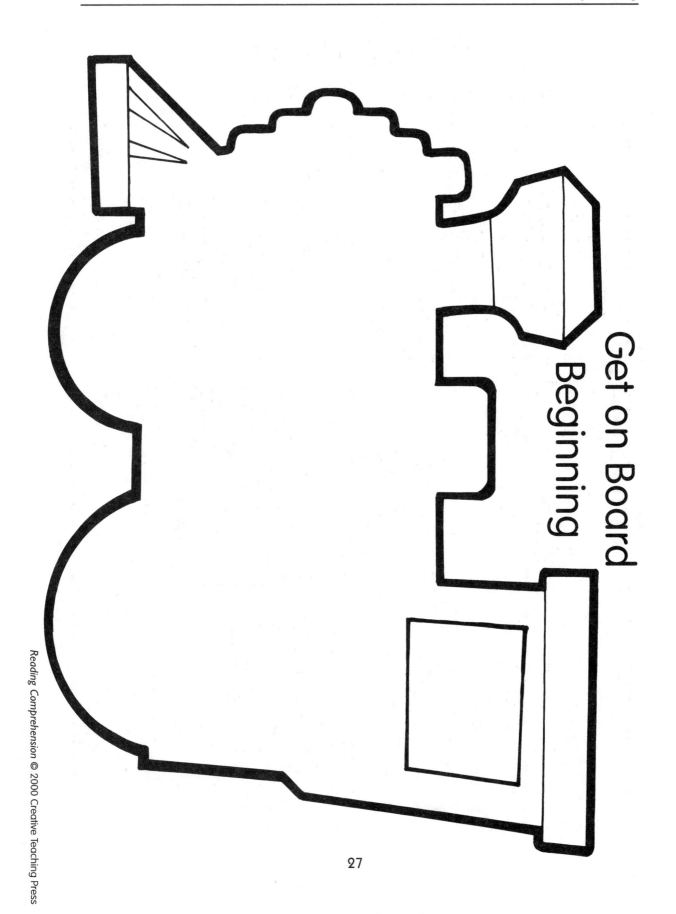

Get on Board
Beginning

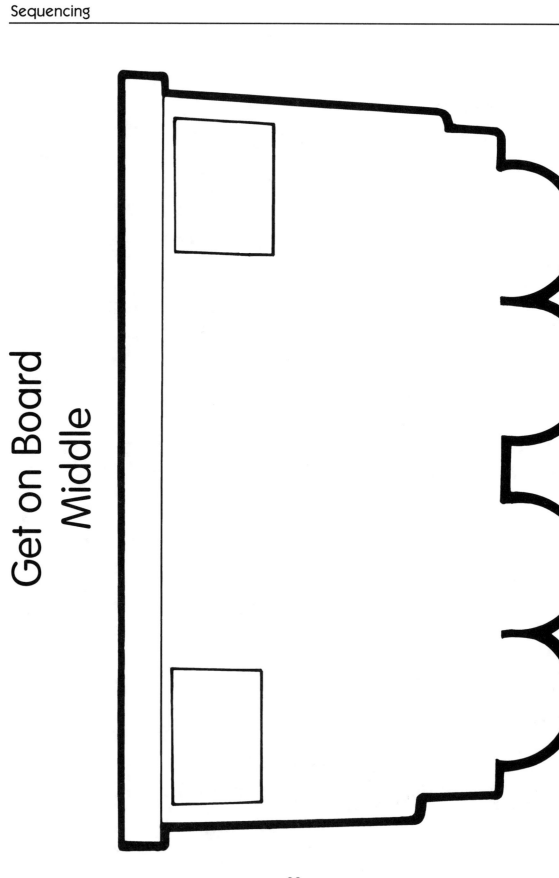

Get on Board
Middle

28

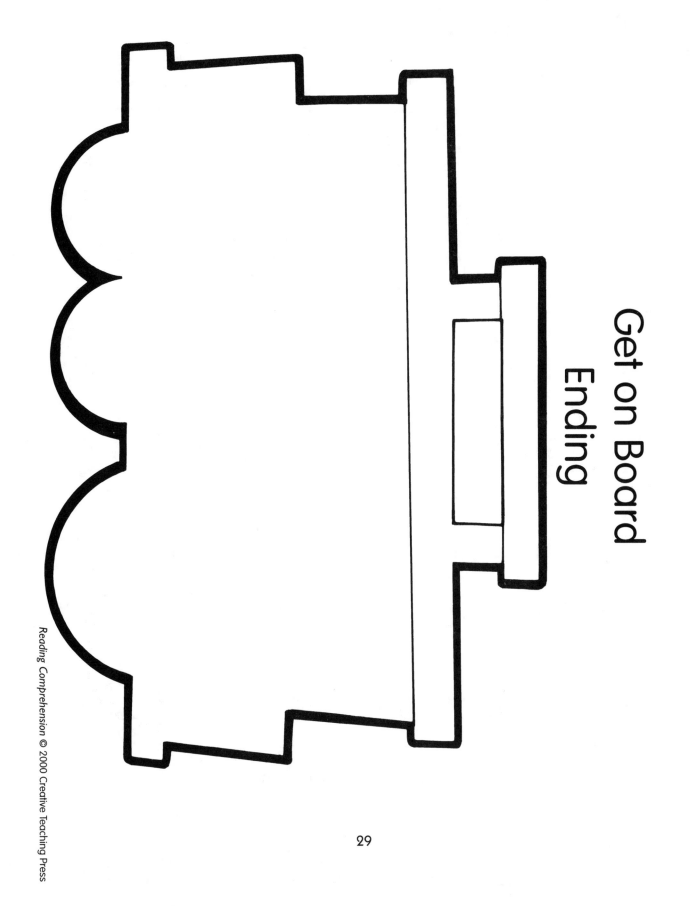

Get on Board
Ending

The Story Train

Materials

- Get on Board reproducibles (pages 27–29)
- Wiggle Caterpillar reproducible (page 31)
- scissors
- card stock
- construction paper (assorted colors)
- glue
- stapler
- paper strips

In advance, make one copy of the Get on Board reproducibles and a class set of the Wiggle Caterpillar reproducible. Cut out each of the train cars, and trace each car several times on card stock. Cut out the cars. Read aloud the Wiggle Caterpillar story. Ask students to identify the beginning, middle, and ending of the story. Next, have students work in small groups and use the train templates to trace each of the three cars on different-colored construction paper. Have students trace the freight car three times on the same color construction paper. Then, ask students to cut out each train car and arrange the five cars on their desk in the correct order, starting with the engine. Tell students that the engine symbolizes the beginning, the freight cars symbolize the middle, and the caboose represents the ending of the story. Next, give each student a copy of the story, and invite students to cut apart the sentences. Have them glue each sentence, in the correct sequence, onto the appropriate train car. Model how to attach neighboring cars together by stapling one end of a paper strip to the back side of each car. Have students take their completed train home to share with their parents.

Student Story Trains

Materials

- Get on Board reproducibles (pages 27–29)
- 3 shoe boxes
- art supplies (e.g., glue, markers, construction paper)
- scissors
- butcher paper
- tape

Make multiple copies of the Get on Board reproducibles. Decorate three shoe boxes, and label them *Beginning, Middle,* and *Ending.* Place the shoe boxes at a writing center, and fill each box with copies of the corresponding train car reproducible. Invite each student to choose a piece of his or her writing. Have students recopy their story on the train cars, correctly sequencing the events into the beginning, middle, and ending of the story. Then, have students cut out their finished cars. Collect the completed "story trains." Cut strips from butcher paper, and tape them on the walls around your classroom to create a "train track." Tape the story trains on the track for all to enjoy.

Wiggle Caterpillar

Once there was a caterpillar named Wiggle.

Wiggle loved to crawl on the ground and eat leaves.

One day Wiggle felt tired and climbed to a high branch.

He made a soft place to rest called a cocoon.

Wiggle stayed inside for many days and nights.

Then, he struggled and broke free.

Wiggle had changed.

He waved his wings and flew happily away as a beautiful butterfly.

Retelling

What Is the Skill?

Retelling is the ability to summarize and organize the elements of a story. It involves processing the key points of the text and explaining those points in your own words. Good listening skills are an important part of this strategy.

Why Do Students Need to Know It?

Having students retell a story can help you discover what details they focused on while reading. Successful retelling focuses students' attention on the main theme of the story. Students must be able to identify and verbalize the overall picture and then break it down into the important parts. Retelling also requires students to look beyond the trivial details of the story and get to the key elements of the text.

Teaching Tips

Retelling is an important skill for both narrative and expository (nonfiction) text. In retelling a narrative story, a student must be aware of the order in which the events are expressed. The sequencing skills discussed in the Sequencing section (pages 23–31) will help students order events correctly. Expository text is more fact-laden, so retelling may not be as sequential as that of narrative text. In this type of text, students should be "reading to learn," or gaining information not previously known. Give students experiences in retelling both types of text, and discuss the differences with them.

Cue Cards

Materials
- Cue Cards (page 34)
- scissors
- short story

Make one copy of the Cue Cards. Cut apart the cards, and laminate them for durability. Select a short story, and read it aloud. Then, demonstrate a retelling of the story by using the cue cards as a guide. Present the cards in the following order: *Who, When, Where, What, Why,* and *How.* Use them to teach students how to discuss the main characters and setting first, then the main theme of the story, and finally the higher-level issues of how and why. Discuss with students how the cards were helpful in remembering the events of the story.

Partner Reading

Materials
- Cue Cards (page 34)
- The Lost Puppy reproducible (page 35)
- The Wacky Day reproducible (page 36)
- scissors

Make one copy of each reproducible for every two students, and cut apart the cards, or have students cut them apart. Divide the class into pairs. Give each pair one copy of The Lost Puppy reproducible, one copy of The Wacky Day reproducible, and a set of cue cards. Have each partner select one of the stories to read. Have one partner read aloud his or her story and then turn the story facedown on the desk. Have the student use the cue cards as a prompt to retell the story to the listener. Have the listener pay attention to the retelling and make sure all the important elements are addressed. If any are missing, have the listener ask his or her partner to discuss that element. After the retelling is complete, have students switch roles and use the other story to repeat the activity.

Cue Cards

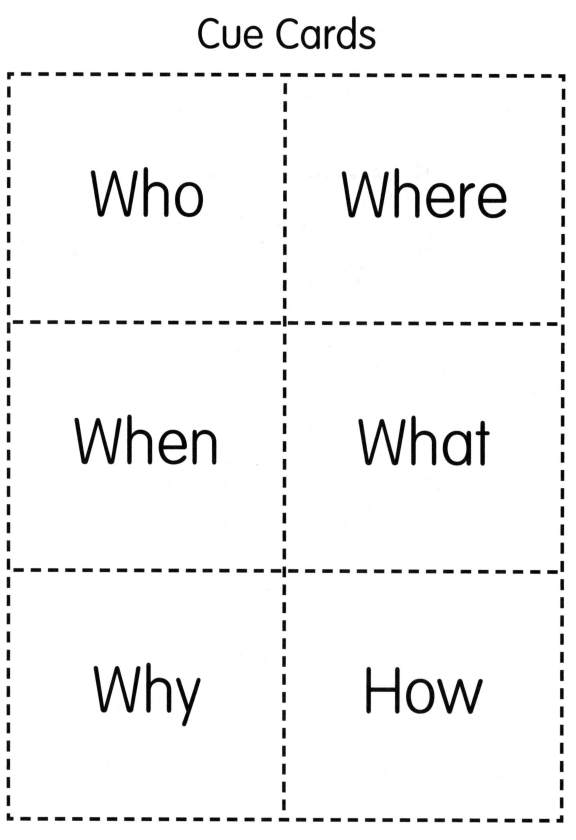

Who

Where

When

What

Why

How

Reading Comprehension © 2000 Creative Teaching Press

The Lost Puppy

On the morning of John's birthday, his family surprised him with a soft, brown puppy. John named the puppy "Willie." Willie slept on John's bed with him every night.

One night, John got ready for bed and called to Willie to come to his room. Willie didn't come, and this made John worry. He searched his entire house, but there was no sign of his puppy. John and his family looked everywhere for Willie. They called his name and offered treats, but Willie still didn't come. They were all beginning to worry.

Then suddenly they heard a quiet sound. It was the sound of Willie crying! They followed the sound to a large laundry basket in the bathroom. There was Willie!

"How did he get in there?" asked John.

"He must have jumped in and flipped it over on top of him," said his father.

John said, "You poor thing! Let's go to bed. I'm so glad that we found you!"

The Wacky Day

The morning bell rang and the students lined up to go to their classroom. Their teacher opened the door to find a shocking sight. The tables and chairs were upside down and their school supplies were hanging from the ceiling!

The teacher said, "This is strange! What has happened to our classroom?"

The students had no idea. They had never seen such a thing before. They walked through the door and stared at the wacky sight.

The class called the principal to come and see their room. When she arrived, all she could do was laugh.

"What a funny sight! I wonder who did this. I guess it is a mystery!" said the principal.

The students were confused. Why didn't their principal seem upset by the messy room? As the principal walked past them, they noticed that she was wearing her clothes inside out. What a wacky day!

Be the Teacher

Materials

- class set of expository books or nonfiction articles

Give each student a different expository book or nonfiction article to read. Have each student read the selection and prepare a short oral report that retells the important information. Explain to students that they will be responsible for teaching their classmates about the information they have read. Have students pay attention to facts that are important to the meaning of the text and ignore the unimportant information. Give students an opportunity to make a visual aide for the retelling, such as a chart, a diagram, or a flowchart, to help them remember key details from the text. Invite each student to present his or her retelling to the class, and invite classmates to ask questions about the presentation.

Sandwich Making

Materials

- jam
- paper cups
- bread
- craft sticks
- paper plates

In advance, put a small scoop of jam in a paper cup for each student. Give each student a piece of bread, a cup of jam, a craft stick, and a paper plate. Ask students to make a sandwich and display it on their plate the way they like to eat it best (e.g., cut into four pieces, cut in two pieces, uncut, rolled). Have students use the craft stick as a knife. Then, pair each student with a partner. Give each student a second set of materials to use in the retelling phase of the activity. Have one partner retell to the other the process he or she used to make the sandwich. Ask the listener to follow the directions given by the teller to make a sandwich the same way. Have the teller monitor his or her retelling by how well the listener is able to correctly re-create the sandwich. Ask partners to switch roles and repeat the activity. Use the sandwiches for a special picnic lunch to celebrate the retelling practice.

Predicting

What Is the Skill?

Predicting involves thinking about what is known in the text and anticipating what will happen next. There are no wrong answers in predicting. The accuracy of the prediction will become evident when the next section of text is read.

Why Do Students Need to Know It?

Making predictions helps to engage the student in the text. Students begin to connect the information in the text with their real-life experiences. Predicting also gives students a chance to extend their imaginations. The more experience they have with making predictions, the more they will think creatively of the possibilities that could exist given a set of circumstances. As students read, their predictions will be confirmed or denied, providing them with immediate feedback.

Teaching Tips

One of the biggest challenges in teaching students to make predictions is convincing them that their answers do not need to be "right." Many students will not willingly make predictions because they are afraid that something else will happen in the story. Explain to students that predictions are based on what they have read and/or what they already know. Provide many opportunities for students to make predictions. The more experiences they have, the more comfortable they will be with the process. Finally, model making predictions as you read aloud to students. Be sure to occasionally make incorrect predictions. Tell students that your prediction could have occurred, but with the new information presented in the next section of text, you see that it did not.

Pointers for Predicting

Materials
- Pointers for Predicting reproducible (page 40)
- Prediction Log (page 41)
- poster board

Copy the tips from the Pointers for Predicting reproducible onto poster board, and hang it in a prominent place. Make a class set of the two reproducibles, and give each student a copy. Use the information presented below to introduce each tip to students. Invite students to keep the reproducibles in a reading folder. Have students practice using these tips before and during their reading.

- Invite students to first read the title of their book or story. Have them consider what clues the title provides about the topic of the text. Can a prediction be made about the characters, setting, or problem based on the title alone?
- Tell students to take a "picture walk" before reading. Invite them to look through the entire selection and take a moment to study each picture. Have students think about the actions shown in the pictures and determine if the pictures provide clues about what might be in the text. If students are reading expository text, have them review any charts and diagrams to look for clues about the topic.
- Have students think about the topic of the book or story. For example, if students are reading a fairy tale, have them consider other fairy tales they may know. If students are reading a book about rockets, have them consider what they know about space and space travel. Using their background knowledge of a topic will enable them to make more reasonable predictions about unfamiliar text.
- Encourage students to record their predictions as they read. Have students use the Prediction Log to help them to look at the predictions they make along the way and then compare their predictions to what is actually happening in the text.

Pointers for Predicting

1. Read the title. Make a prediction.
2. Take a "picture walk."
   - Use the pictures to help you predict what will happen next.
   - Look for visuals like charts, diagrams, and flowcharts to help you make predictions.
3. Compare this story to others you have read that are the same.
4. Record your predictions on the Prediction Log as you read.

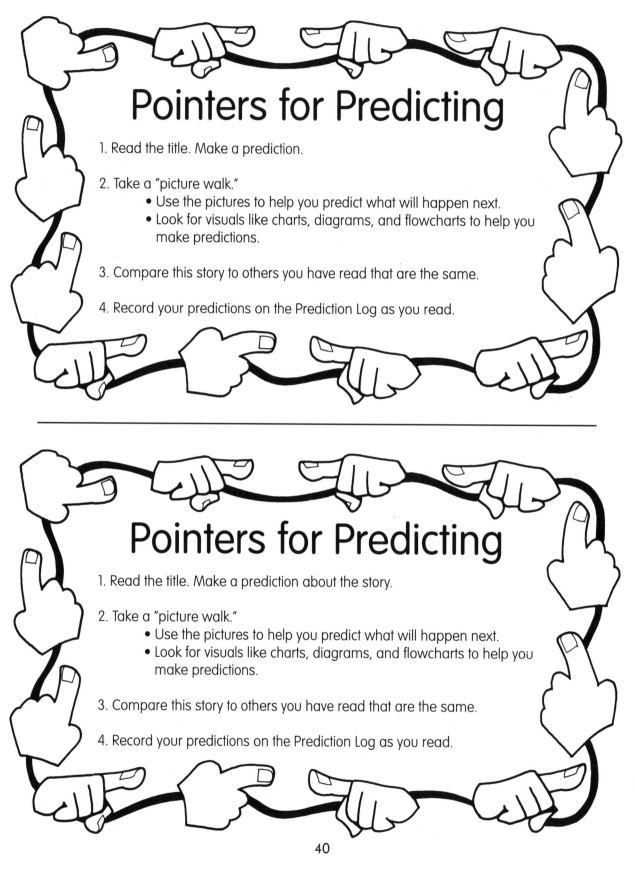

Pointers for Predicting

1. Read the title. Make a prediction.

2. Take a "picture walk."
   • Use the pictures to help you predict what will happen next.
   • Look for visuals like charts, diagrams, and flowcharts to help you make predictions.

3. Compare this story to others you have read that are the same.

4. Record your predictions on the Prediction Log as you read.

Pointers for Predicting

1. Read the title. Make a prediction about the story.

2. Take a "picture walk."
   • Use the pictures to help you predict what will happen next.
   • Look for visuals like charts, diagrams, and flowcharts to help you make predictions.

3. Compare this story to others you have read that are the same.

4. Record your predictions on the Prediction Log as you read.

Prediction Log

Name _____ Date _____

Book Title _____

Directions: Record predictions you make as you read.

I stopped reading on page _____.

I predict _____

_____.

I stopped reading on page _____.

I predict _____

_____.

I stopped reading on page _____.

I predict _____

_____.

I stopped reading on page _____.

I predict _____

_____.

I stopped reading on page _____.

I predict _____

_____.

Reading Comprehension © 2000 Creative Teaching Press

Prediction Points

Materials

- reading materials

Teach students to become physically involved in making predictions. Have them listen carefully as you read aloud. When they formulate a prediction about what will happen next in the story, have them raise their hand and point their index finger to the sky. Call this a "prediction point." Invite students to share their predictions with the class. Always ask students to assess if the prediction is possible, given what they know about the text. Remind students that predictions come from what they have learned from the text and what they already know about the topic. Having students keep these guidelines in mind will help avoid outrageous guesses that disrupt the flow of the lesson.

Prediction Pit Stops

Materials

- age-appropriate book or story
- chart paper
- paper

In advance, choose an age-appropriate book, and divide it into three sections. Select breaks in the story that will allow for students to make predictions about what will happen next. Read aloud the story until you reach the first break. Tell students you are taking a "prediction pit stop." Ask students to share the facts they have learned to this point in the story. Record their answers on a piece of chart paper. Review the facts, and ask each student to write on a piece of paper a prediction about what will happen next. Then, continue reading, and stop at the next break to make another prediction pit stop. Ask students to check their prediction from the first section, and discuss their accuracy. Have students share the new information they learned in the second section of text, and record this on a new piece of chart paper. Again, ask students to make a prediction on their own paper. Finish reading the story, and have students compare their prediction to what actually happened. Spend time discussing student predictions. Refer students to the facts recorded on the chart paper, and discuss how the facts provided clues to what happened next in the story. Try this activity with both narrative and expository text. Continue to encourage students to use what they read to improve their predictions.

Prediction Pyramid

Materials
- Prediction Pyramid reproducible (page 44)
- story

In advance, choose a story to read aloud. Then, select eight words from the story that correspond to the categories on the Prediction Pyramid reproducible. Print the words you select on the lines at the top of the pyramid, and make a class set of the reproducible. Then, give each student a copy of the pyramid. Read aloud each word, and discuss any words that are new or unfamiliar. Next, read together the categories on the pyramid, and have student volunteers explain each one. Ask students to predict how each word at the top of the reproducible will be used in the story and write it in that category space on the pyramid. Then, read aloud the story. Ask students to listen for the special words as you read. When you finish the story, invite students to share their predictions with the class and compare them with the actual events in the story. Try this activity several times, and have students assess how their prediction skills improve.

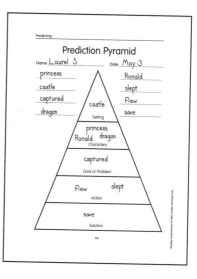

Vocabulary Predictor

Materials
- science or social studies chapter
- sentence strips
- paper
- tape
- journals

Choose a chapter that you will be studying from your science or social studies curriculum. Make a list of all the new vocabulary words. Write each word on a separate sentence strip. Organize the class into groups of two or three, and give each group one strip. Have the group members make a prediction about what their word might mean and how it will be used in the lesson. Invite each group to select one member as a recorder. Have the recorder write down the group's prediction on a piece of paper. Collect the sentence strips, and hang them on a word wall or bulletin board. Post each prediction paper under the corresponding sentence strip. Then, refer to the words as you study them in the chapter. Invite group members to share their prediction about the new word, and compare that prediction to what is learned in the chapter. Add new words to the display as you introduce new vocabulary. Have students make their own predictions about what the words mean and record them in their journal for that curriculum area.

Prediction Pyramid

Name _____   Date _____

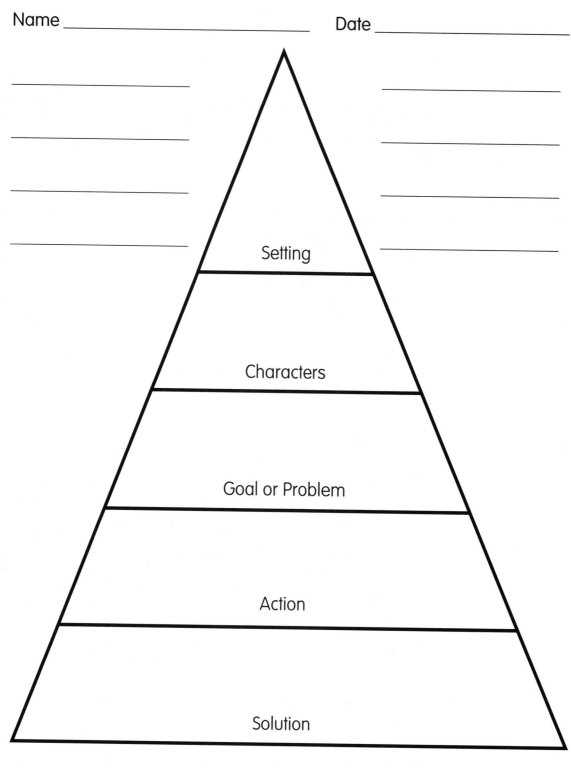

Setting

Characters

Goal or Problem

Action

Solution

Reading Comprehension © 2000 Creative Teaching Press

Accessing Prior Knowledge

What Is the Skill?

Prior knowledge is what we already know or have experienced. When reading, we need to tap into this knowledge in order to make sense of new information. This skill is especially important when reading expository text. We have an existing knowledge base on which to build with the new information being presented.

Why Do Students Need to Know It?

Research shows a strong correlation between accessing prior knowledge and improved reading comprehension. Students with prior knowledge of a topic, who think about that knowledge before reading a book, tend to read more efficiently and have a greater understanding of the material presented. It follows that students with no prior knowledge or experience with a topic will often have no basis for relating the concepts and vocabulary presented. The result is often that students struggle to move beyond the basic skills of decoding and, therefore, never reach the higher-level comprehension skills necessary for learning to take place.

Teaching Tips

Assist students in learning to access their prior knowledge by giving them many opportunities to connect what they read to what they already know. If students have no prior knowledge of a particular topic, present opportunities for them to gain some. For example, if students are reading a book titled *A Day at the Beach* and they have no knowledge of the beach, they may have difficulty comprehending the story. To make the process easier, bring in beach-related objects, show videos of the beach, or introduce new vocabulary by relating it to pictures in the text. Students will find greater success in comprehending what they read when they have a basis for relating new information.

Story Mapping

Materials

- Story Map (page 47)
- story
- chart paper
- colored markers
- selected readings
- glue
- construction paper

In advance, select a story to read aloud. Make a class set of the Story Map, and copy the map onto chart paper. Write the topic of the story in the center square of the map. Display the story map for all students to see. Ask students if they know anything about the topic in the center of the chart. Use a marker to record their responses in the circles around the topic. (Include all answers—even if some are incorrect. Incorrect responses will be addressed after the story has been read.) Add more circles as needed to record student responses. Next, read aloud the story. Conduct a postreading discussion to check the information on the story map. Use a different-colored marker to record any additional information that students learn from the story. Note any information that was found to be incorrect based on the story, and cross it off the chart. Next, give each student a story map. Assign a story from your reading program, or invite each student to select a book of his or her own. Ask each student to complete a story map before reading the selection. Have students add additional circles as needed. Check each student's chart to confirm an understanding of the skill. Have students glue their finished story map to construction paper, and display the maps around the classroom.

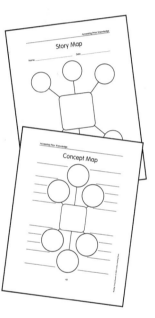

Concept Mapping

Materials

- Concept Map (page 48)
- science or social studies chapter
- butcher paper

Select a chapter from your science or social studies curriculum. Make a class set of the Concept Map, and copy the map onto a large piece of butcher paper. Hang the butcher paper on a bulletin board. Write the concept or topic of the chapter in the center square of the concept map, and write subtopics in the circles around the square. Conduct a class discussion about each subtopic. Record students' prior knowledge about each subtopic on the lines around the circles. Add additional lines as needed. Refer to the bulletin board display as the class studies the chapter. Add new information that students learn, and cross out information found to be incorrect in the text. Use the completed concept map as a tool for review at the end of the chapter.

Story Map

Name _____ Date _____

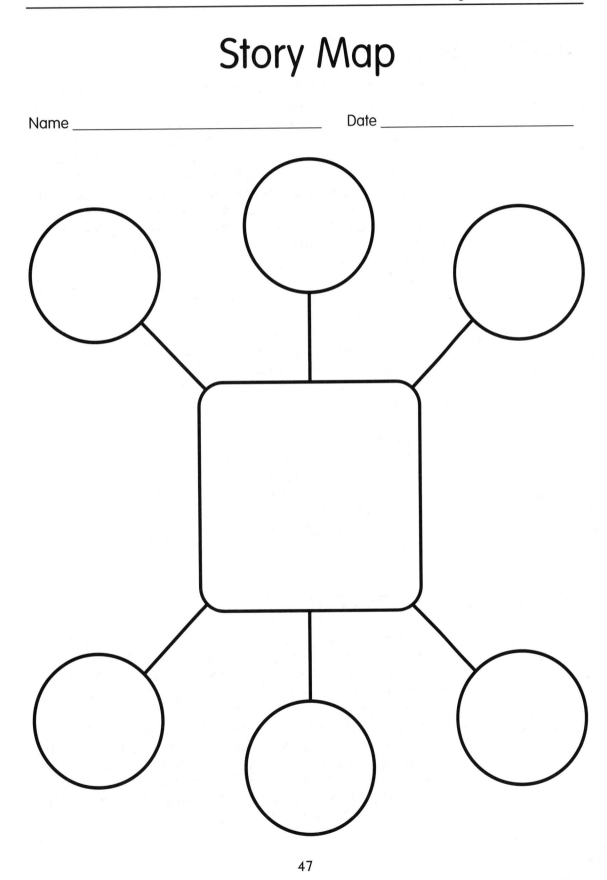

Concept Map

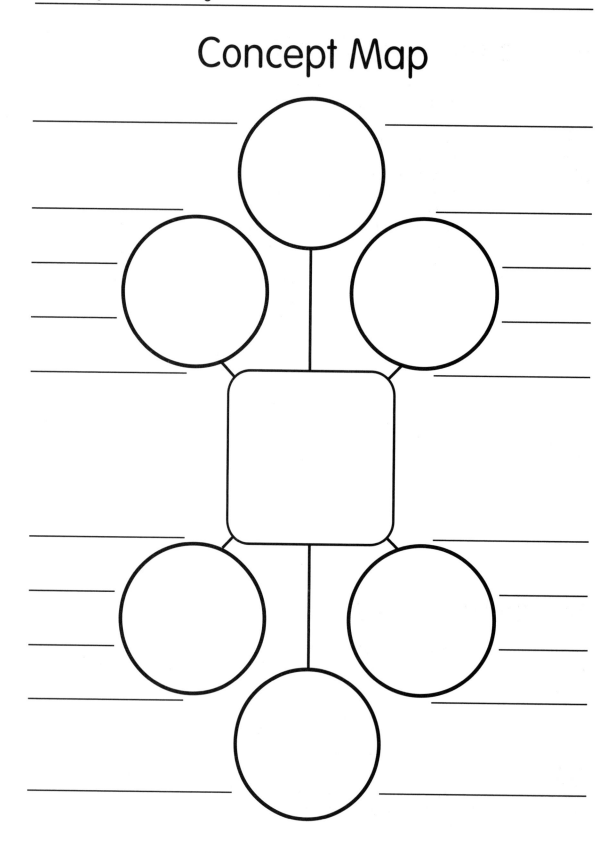

48

Inside/Outside Circles

Materials

- Inside/Outside Circles reproducible (page 50)
- butcher paper
- book

Copy the graphic organizer from the Inside/Outside Circles reproducible onto a piece of butcher paper. Change the heading of the outside circle to read *What We Learned* and the heading of the inside circle to read *What We Know.* Select a book to read aloud. Begin by writing the topic or theme of the book at the top of the butcher paper. Ask students to share what they know about this topic. Record their answers inside the inner circle. Read aloud the book, and then have students review the *What We Know* circle. Invite student volunteers to share the new information they learned from the book. Write this information in the ring between the inner and outer circle. Try to fill the space if possible. Then, invite students to review both circles. Show them how much their knowledge grew after reading the book by pointing out the information written in the outer circle. Display the chart in the classroom for students to refer to as they complete their own Inside/Outside Circles.

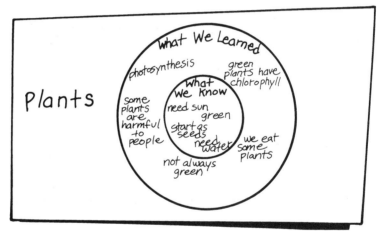

Student Circles

Materials

- Inside/Outside Circles reproducible (page 50)
- age-appropriate book or textbook
- glue
- construction paper

Make a class set of the Inside/Outside Circles reproducible. Have each student select a book to read independently, or assign a passage from a textbook. Have each student write on the reproducible the topic of his or her book or passage. Ask students to spend a few minutes completing the inner circle of their reproducible with all the information they already know about their topic. Next, ask students to read their selection. Then, have them complete the *What I Learned* section of their paper. Discuss student responses as a class. Glue the completed reproducibles to construction paper, and use them to create a bulletin board display around the large inside/outside circles made by the whole class.

Inside/Outside Circles

Name _____   Date _____

Book Title _____   Topic _____

Directions: List what you know about your topic in the inner circle. Read your book, and then record what you learned in the outer circle.

What I Learned

What I Know

Reading Comprehension © 2000 Creative Teaching Press

As Bright as the Sun

Materials

- yellow butcher paper
- magnets, magnetic tape, or tape
- age-appropriate book
- scissors

Draw a large circle on a piece of yellow butcher paper. Around the circle add eight triangles to create a sun. Use magnets or magnetic tape to attach the sun to the chalkboard, or tape it to a wall. Select a book to read aloud to students, and write the topic of the book in the center of the circle before the lesson. Invite students to share with you all the information they know about the topic. Write their responses on the circle around the topic. Read the book aloud. After you finish reading, ask students what new information they learned. Write their responses on the rays, or triangles, around the sun. Write one response on each ray. If you receive more responses than there are rays, add more than one answer to each triangle. Then, direct students' attention to the amount of new information they learned from the book. Cut out the sun, and hang it in the classroom, or use it as a part of the bulletin board described in the next activity.

Our Reading Garden

Materials

- sun from As Bright as the Sun activity
- Our Reading Garden reproducible (page 52)
- copy paper (assorted colors)
- scissors
- independent-reading books
- glue
- markers
- stapler

Make a class set of the Our Reading Garden reproducible on several different colors of copy paper. Have each student select a reproducible and cut out the circle and petal shapes. Next, have students select a book for independent reading. Before they begin to read, ask students to write the topic of their book in the middle of their circle piece. Assist students who may have difficulty identifying their topic. Then, have students write everything they know about their topic in the space remaining on the circle. Next, have students read their book and write new information they learn on each petal piece. Invite students to glue their petals to the back of their circle to create a flower. Use the flowers to decorate a bulletin board display titled *Our Reading Garden.* Invite students to use markers to draw stems and leaves. Staple the sun from the previous activity to the top of the display. Encourage students to add additional flowers as they read more books.

Our Reading Garden

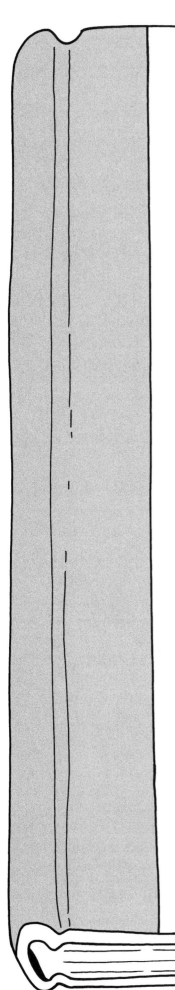

Characterization

What Is the Skill?

Understanding the characters in a story is an important part of comprehending the text. This understanding must go beyond merely naming the characters. Deeper understanding involves recognizing the traits of the characters, understanding what they do and why, and identifying their role in the overall meaning of the story. Characterization is typically a skill most useful in narrative text, but the same need for understanding is present when studying biographies or individuals in history.

Why Do Students Need to Know It?

Much of what is learned about a story comes through the eyes, ears, and thoughts of the characters. Getting to know the characters enables students to understand the book at a deeper level. Being able to identify character traits helps students find similarities and differences between the characters and themselves. These comparisons bring the text to a more personal level for students, helping them to learn more about themselves through the pages of the books they read.

Teaching Tips

Choosing literature selections with many interesting characters will help to motivate students' desire to learn. Provide students with a variety of opportunities to think about the characters outside of the story. Use the suggestions presented in this section to develop students' ability to understand the characters they read about.

Mail Time

Materials

- fairy tales
- writing paper
- envelopes
- art supplies (e.g., markers, paint, brushes, glue)
- shoe box
- scissors

Invite each student to select a favorite fairy tale and reread it. Ask students to imagine that one of the characters wants to write a letter to another character in the story. Have them think about what might be in the letter. For example, in the story *Goldilocks and the Three Bears,* Goldilocks could write to tell the bears that she is sorry for making a mess of their house. Discuss other possible stories and what the characters in those tales might wish to say to each other. Have students choose two characters from their favorite fairy tale and write a letter from one to the other. Remind them to use what they know about the characters when they write their letter. Have students fold their completed letter and place it in an envelope. Ask students to mark the envelope with the name of the character to receive it and an imaginary address. Have students include their own name on the back of the envelope. Decorate a shoe box, and cut a slit in the top. Use the box as a mailbox, and have students place their letter inside. Then, periodically select a letter from the box, and ask the student writer to read it for the class. Invite the class to discuss how the characters writing and receiving each letter might feel.

Reading Riddle

Materials

- reading selection
- index cards

Select a story with several characters from your reading program. Read aloud the story as students follow along, or do a shared reading as a class. Then, pair each student with a partner. Have each student silently select his or her favorite character from the story. Invite students to write down three clues about their character on an index card. (They may need to refer back to the text for assistance.) Next, have partners face each other. Invite one student to begin by reading his or her clues. Have the partner guess which character is being described. Allow students to refer back to the text when making their guesses as well. After the character is correctly identified, have the partners switch roles.

Descriptive Characters

Materials
- reading selection
- newsprint

Select a story to read with the class. Provide all students with a copy of the text so they can follow along. Read aloud the story, and write the name of a main character from the story on the chalkboard. Pair each student with a partner, and give each pair a piece of newsprint. Have one partner copy the character's name on the top of the paper. Next, ask partners to fold their paper in half and each select one side of the paper on which to write. Have one student begin by writing on his or her side of the paper a word that describes the main character. Then, have the partner write a different describing word on his or her side. Have partners alternate back and forth, adding new words to the paper. If they have difficulty finding describing words, refer them to the text for more ideas. When neither student can think of any more ideas, have partners raise their hands. Review the pair's list, and assist them in finding more describing words if their list seems incomplete. Then, have pairs share with the class some of the describing words they wrote. Try this activity with other characters from the same story, or choose a new story. Extend this activity by making it a game. Have pairs try to find the most words to describe their character. Count each pair's words at the end of a set time limit, and award a pat on the back to the winning pair.

Hot Seat

Materials
- sentence strip
- tape
- reading selection

In advance, write *hot seat* on a sentence strip, and tape it to a chair. Select a story that has several characters, and provide all students with a copy of the text. Read aloud the story. Choose one character, and ask for a student volunteer to pretend to be that character. Invite the student volunteer to sit in the "hot seat" at the front of the room. Have the other students ask the "character" questions about events that happened in the story and questions that move beyond literal facts. Have students include questions about how the character might have felt or why the character may have made certain decisions. (Most of these types of questions will not have a right or wrong answer. If the student volunteer has difficulty answering, remind him or her of facts from the story that might give clues to the character's traits.) Try the hot seat with different characters from the story, and allow more than one student to play the same character.

Character Collage

Materials

- construction paper
- magazines
- scissors
- glue

Ask each student to select a character from a book or story that he or she has recently read. Give each student a piece of construction paper and a magazine. Have students write the name of their character in the center of the construction paper. Then, have students look through their magazine to find pictures and words that they think represent their character. Invite students to cut out these images and words and glue them on the construction paper around the name of their character. Have students fill the page with images to create a collage. Give each student an opportunity to share his or her collage with the class. Hang the finished collages around the classroom for all to enjoy.

Favorite Character Award

Materials

- Favorite Character Award (page 57)
- reading selections
- crayons or markers
- glue
- construction paper

Give each student a copy of the Favorite Character Award. Have each student select his or her favorite character from a book or story. Invite students to use information about their character to complete the reproducible. Have students refer back to the text of the book or story for specific details about their character. Ask students to include a drawing of their character on the award. Then, have students glue the award on a piece of construction paper. Hang the awards in your classroom, or create a gallery walk by displaying the awards in a hallway.

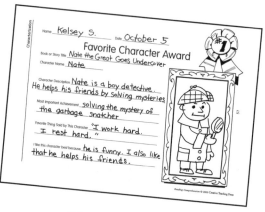

Favorite Character Award

Name _____ Date _____

Book or Story Title _____

Character Name _____

Character Description _____

Most Important Achievement _____

Favorite Thing Said by This Character _____

I like this character best because _____

Draw a picture of your character.

Categorization

What Is the Skill?

Creating categories involves placing things or ideas into groups based on how they are similar. Organizing the details of a story into categories helps the reader keep track of what is important and determine how the pieces of the story fit together.

Why Do Students Need to Know It?

Students need to understand how the details in a story work together to support the main idea. Categorizing the details into logical groupings is the first step toward seeing this connection.

Teaching Tips

Begin teaching this skill by giving students categories and having them sort items into those categories. Once students have mastered this idea, provide them with similar items or ideas, and invite them to create the category. This will take students to a more abstract level of thinking. Finally, have them begin categorizing details from text. As students progress through each skill, they will become more confident in their abilities to see connections between elements in a story.

Where Do I Belong?

Materials

- Where Do I Belong? reproducibles (pages 60–61)
- scissors
- sentence strips
- large manila envelope

Prepare this activity for use at a learning center or an independent workstation. Make a copy of the Where Do I Belong? reproducibles. Cut apart the word cards, and laminate them for durability. Then, write each of the following categories on a separate sentence strip: *colors, drinks, animals, directions, vegetables, fruits, things you wear,* and *games.* Store the word cards and sentence strips in a manila envelope at the center. Include an answer key that shows the correct placement of each word. Invite each student to place all the sentence strips faceup on the desk or table and place the word cards facedown in a pile. Have the student choose one word card at a time and place it under the correct category strip. Ask the student to set aside cards he or she is unsure of and return to those cards later. Then, have the student remove the answer key and check his or her answers. Extend this activity by inviting students to create their own word cards and categories. Pair students with a partner, and have them sort each other's words.

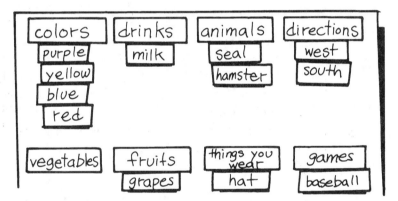

Category Breaks

Materials

- Category Breaks reproducibles (pages 62–63)
- scissors
- container
- paper

Make a copy of the Category Breaks reproducibles. Cut apart the cards, and place them on your desk in a small container labeled *Category Cards.* When you have a free moment between activities, pull a card, and read the three items listed. Ask students to think about the items and try to find a category in which they all belong. (Note that in some cases there may be more than one answer. The category listed on the card is one suggestion.) Ask students to justify their answers. Extend this activity by inviting students to add cards to the container. Leave blank pieces of paper near the container for students to use. Have them write their three items on the paper and include the corresponding category they had in mind. Collect the papers, and add them to the container for future games.

Where Do I Belong?

purple	yellow	blue
red	dog	white
hamster	cat	wolf
banana	grapes	tiger
apple	water	apricot
juice	milk	lemon
soda	coffee	green
seal	pear	lemonade

Reading Comprehension © 2000 Creative Teaching Press

Where Do I Belong?

kick ball	soccer	baseball
tennis	carrot	football
bean	pea	hockey
north	south	east
west	hat	up
shoes	shirt	down
gloves	coat	socks

Category Breaks

lightning thunder rain **category:** weather elements	magenta violet turquoise **category:** colors	two four ten **category:** numbers
paint crayons markers **category:** art supplies	hats cake presents **category:** birthday items	bones food leash **category:** dog items
soda juice water **category:** drinks	paper stamps envelopes **category:** letter-writing supplies	penny nickel dime **category:** money

Reading Comprehension © 2000 Creative Teaching Press

Category Breaks

sight hearing smell **category:** senses	daisy tulip rose **category:** flowers	pants shirt socks **category:** clothing
robin sparrow cardinal **category:** birds	math social studies science **category:** school subjects	vanilla chocolate strawberry **category:** ice-cream flavors
brownie cookie ice cream **category:** desserts	banana orange peach **category:** fruit	carrot broccoli peas **category:** vegetables

Telling Details

Materials

- chart paper
- reading selection
- reading journals

In advance, label three pieces of chart paper *Characters, Setting,* and *Problem.* Hang the charts in the front of the room for all students to see. Choose a story to read aloud, and give each student a copy of the text. Read aloud the story as students follow along. Then, ask students to review the text and find details that fit into each category on the chart paper. Record each student response on the appropriate chart. Use the completed charts to discuss how each element relates to the overall meaning of the story. Have students explain how identifying each element will help to understand the story better. Assist students in writing a description of each of these story elements in a reading journal. Ask students to keep these story elements in mind as they read independently.

Story Elements

Materials

- Story Elements reproducible (page 65)
- overhead transparency/ projector or chart paper
- fairy tale
- reading selections
- scissors
- glue
- construction paper

Make a class set of the Story Elements reproducible, and make one copy on an overhead transparency or chart paper. Select a familiar fairy tale, and fill in the story elements on the transparency or chart paper while you read aloud. Encourage students to look beyond the literal answers and use their background knowledge when thinking about the problem and solution elements. Next, give students a copy of the reproducible to complete on their own. Ask students to select a story for independent reading, or assign a selection from your reading program. Have students read the selection and complete the reproducible. Next, ask students to cut out each story element and glue it to a piece of construction paper. Hang the papers in a hallway, and invite other classes to browse what your students are reading.

Story Elements

Name _____   Date _____

Directions: Read a book of your own. Fill in each story element.

Title

_____

_____

_____

Author

_____

Setting

_____

_____

Characters

_____

_____

Solution

_____

_____

Problem

_____

_____

_____

Identifying the Main Idea

What Is the Skill?

Identifying the main idea involves determining the focus or theme of a story. This requires being able to see how the details of the story work together to support one idea.

Why Do Students Need to Know It?

Finding the main idea is an essential skill of comprehension. Students must be able to identify the main idea in order to understand the message of the text. Knowing the main idea also helps students to use the information in the text. If a selection focuses on the jobs people hold in a community, students will know to use that information when they are asked to discuss community roles.

Teaching Tips

Before students can identify the main idea, they need to understand how to categorize the details in the story. The previous section presented ways to prepare students for this skill. Their ability to analyze the details in the story will help them to attend to the explicit information given. Students can use this information to decide what the main idea is. Model finding the main idea as you read aloud. Challenge students to summarize what happened in a story in a single sentence. Most importantly, provide students with many opportunities to think about the main idea when they read.

Classroom News

Materials

- Classroom News reproducible (page 68)
- overhead transparency/ projector
- class news folders

Make an overhead transparency of the Classroom News reproducible, and give each student a new copy of the reproducible at the beginning of each week. Each morning, invite one student to come to the front of the classroom and share an important piece of news (e.g., lost tooth, family vacation, new baby). Encourage the student to provide details. Allow the rest of the class to ask questions about the news. Model paraphrasing the main idea of the student's news for the first week of the activity. For example, say *Mary and her family had a great vacation at the beach.* Explain to students that you are listening to all the details and using them to summarize the most important information. Write a single sentence about the main idea under the appropriate day on the transparency. Have students write the sentence on their own copy of the reproducible. Invite students to keep the reproducible in a class news folder at their desk so it will be easily accessible each morning. Give students an opportunity to grasp the idea of paraphrasing the main idea, and then invite student volunteers to provide a "main-idea sentence" for the daily news. Finally, allow students to write their own main-idea sentences without assistance. Collect the reproducibles each week to check student work. Have students take home their reproducible at the end of the week to share classroom news with their parents.

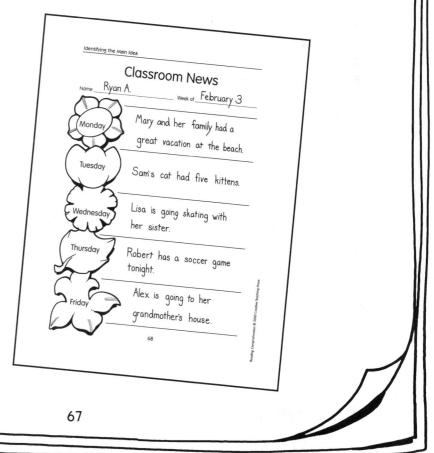

Classroom News

Name _____ Week of _____

Story Coding

Materials

- Story Coding reproducible (page 70)
- overhead transparency/ projector
- red and blue overhead markers

Make an overhead transparency of the Story Coding reproducible. Show students the story on the overhead, and read it aloud. Then, have students read the story with you. Ask students to tell you what they think the story is about. Then, ask for a student volunteer to find one sentence in the paragraph that gives the main idea. Refer students to the first sentence of the paragraph if they need assistance. Lead students to see that the remaining sentences provide details that support this main idea. Code the sentence by underlining the main-idea sentence with a red marker and each supporting detail with a blue marker. Have students use these sentences to paraphrase what the main idea and supporting details are, and write their responses in the appropriate place underneath the story.

What's My Main Idea?

Materials

- sentence strips

In advance, write a three- or four-sentence paragraph that does not have a main-idea sentence, or use the sample sentences below. Write the sentences on the chalkboard. Organize students into groups of three or four, and give each group a blank sentence strip. Have the group members read the sentences on the board together and discuss what the sentences have in common. Ask each group to decide on a main-idea sentence for the details and write it on the sentence strip. Then, invite groups to share their main idea with the rest of the class. Ask groups to justify their reasons for writing their main idea. Repeat this activity with a new set of supporting details, or give groups a main idea and have them write the detail sentences.

We went to see the elephants.

I counted four giraffes.

Watching the bears was fun.

Story Coding

Children long ago had to work very hard. They had many chores to do each day. They had to milk the cows, gather the eggs, and put wood on the fire. Then, they went to school just like you and me.

Main idea: _____

Supporting detail: _____

Supporting detail: _____

Supporting detail: _____

70

Main Idea Bridge

Materials
- Main Idea Bridge reproducible (page 72)
- overhead transparency/ projector
- picture book
- reading selections

Make a class set of the Main Idea Bridge reproducible, and make one copy on an overhead transparency. Select a picture book with a limited amount of text and an obvious main idea. Read aloud the book. Then, show students the bridge on the transparency. Explain to students that the details in a story support the main idea in the same way that beams or braces support a bridge. Model how to use the main idea and supporting details from the picture book to fill in the bridge on the overhead transparency. Invite students to assist you. (The graphic may have more or less spaces for details depending on the book you select. Draw additional supports to accommodate more details, and disregard blank supports if there are fewer details in the story.) Discuss the completed graphic organizer, and help students see the connection between the main idea and supporting details. Then, give each student a copy of the reproducible. Assign students a reading selection, or allow them to choose their own book and independently complete a reproducible. Discuss student responses as a class, and place the completed organizers in students' reading portfolios.

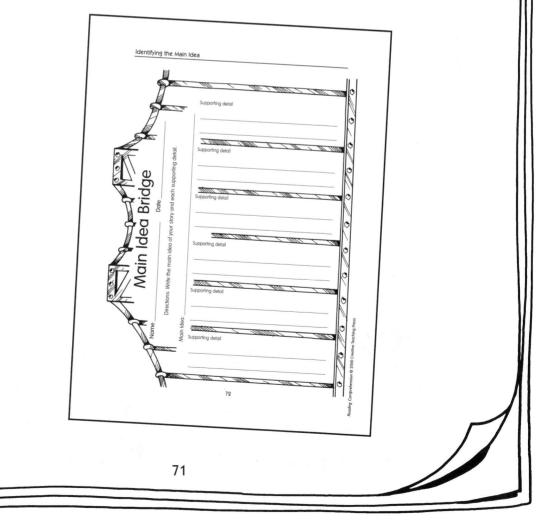

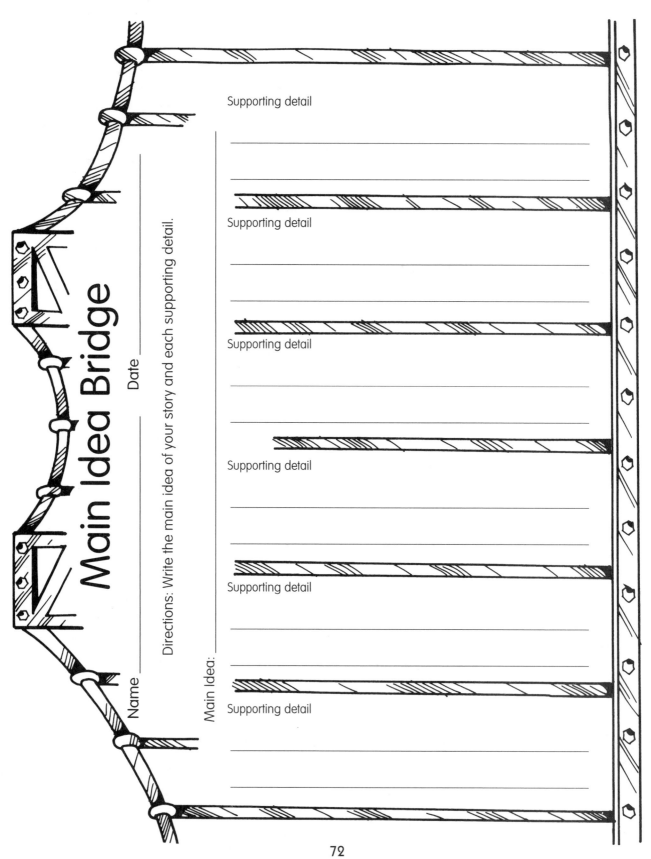

Main Idea Bridge

Name _____

Date _____

Directions: Write the main idea of your story and each supporting detail.

Main Idea: _____

Supporting detail

_____

_____

Supporting detail

_____

_____

Supporting detail

_____

_____

Supporting detail

_____

_____

Supporting detail

_____

_____

Supporting detail

_____

_____

Reading Comprehension © 2000 Creative Teaching Press

Making Inferences

What Is the Skill?

Making inferences involves using background knowledge, along with information from the text, to make assumptions about what is *not* written. Often referred to as "reading between the lines," making inferences requires the reader to move beyond the literal level and make judgments about what the text implies.

Why Do Students Need to Know It?

Early in reading instruction, students are taught how to make predictions about what they read. As their comprehension skills improve, they begin to pay attention to the details in the text and associate those details with their background knowledge. Their prediction skills become more refined, and they are able to tackle the more sophisticated skill of making inferences. While making predictions allows students to guess what will happen next in a story, making inferences requires them to make judgments about the story based on what they know and what is presented in the text. The ability to make inferences helps students to understand the story at a deeper level and to see cause and effect relationships in the story.

Teaching Tips

Teach students the difference between literal and higher-level thinking questions. Tell them that paying attention to the text is important because it gives them the building blocks to make their own decisions about what is not explicitly presented. Use the lessons on finding the main idea to help students determine what information they are given and then extend that information to infer what is not told in the story. Use the activities presented in this section to give students a clear understanding of inferences and help them to begin to unlock the underlying meaning in what they read.

Question Sort

Materials
- The Hungry Mouse reproducible (page 75)
- overhead transparency/projector
- paper

Make an overhead transparency of The Hungry Mouse reproducible. Show students the story, and cover the questions at the bottom of the reproducible with a blank piece of paper. Introduce "right-there" questions and "in-your-head" questions to students. Tell students the answer to a right-there question can be found written in the text. Explain that an in-your-head question requires them to combine what they know from the story with what they know from their own experiences to find the answer. Read aloud the story as students follow along. Next, show students each question, one at a time. Have students point to their desk if the question is a right-there question and point to their head if it is an in-your-head question. Discuss student responses, and ask for student volunteers to explain how they determined the type of each question. Encourage students to think about how the two questions were answered differently.

The Question Game

Materials
- reading selections
- overhead transparency/projector
- paper
- pencils

In advance, select several short stories to read aloud. Try finding simple stories from your reading program. Make an overhead transparency of each story. Organize students into small groups, and give each group a piece of paper and a pencil. Select one story, display the transparency, and read it aloud as students follow along. Then, have each group work together to write three right-there questions and three in-your-head questions about the story. Encourage groups to refer to the text on the overhead as they develop their questions. When all groups are finished, invite one group at a time to read its questions. Have the members of the other groups make guesses about which kind of question is being asked. Encourage group members to think creatively, especially for the in-your-head questions. Use as many stories for this group activity as time will permit. Vary this activity by having each group write as many right-there and in-your-head questions as it can for each story. Then, tally the totals of each kind of question written by each group. Keep score to see which group writes the most questions.

The Hungry Mouse

A little mouse was very hungry. He looked everywhere for something to eat. He loved to eat cheese, crackers, and bread. His favorite food was cookies. The little mouse hoped to find some tasty cookies in the trash can, but it was empty. He checked the cupboards, but everything was sealed shut. The poor little mouse was about to give up when he saw a piece of cookie under the stove. He climbed up the stove and nibbled on the cookie. After eating it all up, he went to find a soft, safe place to take a nap.

1. What was the mouse's favorite food?
2. Where did the mouse live?
3. What did the mouse love to eat?
4. In what room was the mouse looking for food?
5. Do you think the people in this house knew about the mouse?
6. Where did the mouse look for his food?
7. Do you think the mouse had enough to eat? Why or why not?

Reading Comprehension © 2000 Creative Teaching Press

The Picture Says

Materials

- wordless picture books
- paper
- pencils

Divide the class into groups of three. Give each group a wordless picture book. Have students in each group look through their book and discuss the story told by the pictures. Remind students that because there is no text, they will need to infer what the illustrator is trying to express. Give the groups about 15 to 20 minutes to review the book and make some notes about the story. Then, invite groups to retell their story for the class. Have groups show the pictures from their book as they speak. Ask students to justify the inferences they made about their book.

If–Then

Materials

- drawing paper
- crayons or markers

Remind students of the differences between making an inference and stating a fact. (Review the right-there questions and the in-your-head questions introduced in the Question Sort activity on page 74.) Next, introduce the concepts of *cause* and *effect.* Tell students that a *cause* is an event or action that occurs and an *effect* is what happens as a result of the cause. Provide examples as necessary. Then, give each student a piece of drawing paper. Have students fold their paper in half and then open the paper up again. On the left side of the paper, have students write an "if" statement (e.g., *If I ride my bike in the rain*) at the top. On the top right side of the paper, have students write a resulting "then" statement that would logically follow (e.g., *then I will get wet*). Have students draw a picture that represents each statement in the space below. Post the drawings on a bulletin board display featuring cause and effect.

Face the Facts

Materials

- Face the Facts reproducible (page 78)
- Fact Cards (page 79)
- overhead transparency/projector
- paper
- scissors
- small box

Make an overhead transparency of the Face the Facts reproducible, and photocopy a class set of the Fact Cards. Show students the Face the Facts transparency, and direct their attention to the first box. Cover the last two boxes with a blank piece of paper. Read the three fact statements in the first box, and then read the inference questions. Ask students to respond to the questions based on the facts given. Discuss how different answers may be possible as long as they make sense with the facts provided. Follow the same procedure for the remaining two boxes. Next, give each student a copy of the Fact Cards. Ask students to write three related facts in the first box. Have students refer to the examples for help. Then, have students write an in-your-head question about the three facts at the bottom of the box. Walk around the room to check students' work. Assist students who are having difficulty. When all students understand the concept, invite them to complete the remaining two boxes on the reproducible. Then, ask students to cut apart the boxes to create cards. Collect all the cards, and place them in a box on your desk labeled *Fact Cards.* When you have a free moment between activities, or at the beginning or end of the day, pull a card, and read the three facts. Ask the inference question, and invite student volunteers to suggest possible answers. Have the writer of the card explain the answer he or she had in mind as well.

Face the Facts

Fact 1: You are at home and it is lunchtime.
Fact 2: You are hungry and want to make a sandwich.
Fact 3: The meat has to be stored in a cold place.

In-Your-Head Questions
      Where would you look to find the meat? Why?

Fact 1: James put on his bathing suit.
Fact 2: He called his friends to make plans.
Fact 3: He grabbed his towel and left the house.

In-Your-Head Questions
      Where do you think James was going? Why?

Fact 1: Lisa sneezed three times.
Fact 2: Her throat felt scratchy and sore.
Fact 3: She had soccer practice after school.

In-Your-Head Questions
      What do you think Lisa will do after school? Why?

Reading Comprehension © 2000 Creative Teaching Press

Fact Cards

Directions: Write three related facts and an in-your-head question.

Fact 1: _____

Fact 2: _____

Fact 3: _____

In-Your-Head Question

_____

Directions: Write three related facts and an in-your-head question.

Fact 1: _____

Fact 2: _____

Fact 3: _____

In-Your-Head Question

_____

Directions: Write three related facts and an in-your-head question.

Fact 1: _____

Fact 2: _____

Fact 3: _____

In-Your-Head Question

_____

Making Connections

What Is the Skill?

In order for a book to have meaning in our life, we need to connect it to what we know. Learning becomes real when we make connections to our personal experiences. We compare what we read to our own view of ourselves, our perceptions of the world around us, and other things we have read.

Why Do Students Need to Know It?

Students who are learning to read may have a limited understanding of abstract ideas. In order for them to comprehend what they read, they need to have a way to connect these ideas to what is concrete in their world. Making connections helps students develop an appreciation of reading and an understanding of how things are related.

Teaching Tips

Begin asking students to connect what they read to themselves. Primary-grade students will find an infinite number of ways that they are alike and different from the characters they read about. Build on this personal connection by asking students to compare what they read with what they know of the world. When students are comfortable making this connection, begin to introduce the idea that books may be related to each other. Always make it a point to model connections you observe as you read aloud to students. Vocalize your thought process, and invite students to expand the connections that you note.

Character Connections

Materials
- Character Connections reproducible (page 82)
- overhead transparency/ projector
- reading selection

Make a class set of the Character Connections reproducible, and make one copy on an overhead transparency. Select a story to read aloud that contains at least one strong character with whom you can personally identify. Read aloud the story. Discuss the selected character's traits with students, and talk about similarities between the character and yourself. Record similarities on the transparency as you mention them. Then, give each student a copy of the reproducible. Have students select a familiar character from a recently read story and compare that character to themselves. Encourage students to look deeper than physical characteristics and actions and focus on personality traits and feelings presented in the story. Invite students to draw a self-portrait and the character they chose at the top of the reproducible. Then, have students list four things they have in common with their character. Hang the completed reproducibles on a bulletin board display titled *Connecting to the Characters.*

My Best Friend

Materials
- student journals
- crayons or markers

Have students choose the character from a book or story that they would most like to have as a friend. Ask students to imagine spending the day with this character. Have them think about what they would most like to do and why. Invite students to write a journal entry describing the day and include illustrations of their adventures with the character. Ask students to share their journal entry with a classmate, or invite students to share the events of their special day with the whole class.

Character Connections

Name _____   Date _____

Draw a picture
of yourself.

Draw a picture
of the character you chose.

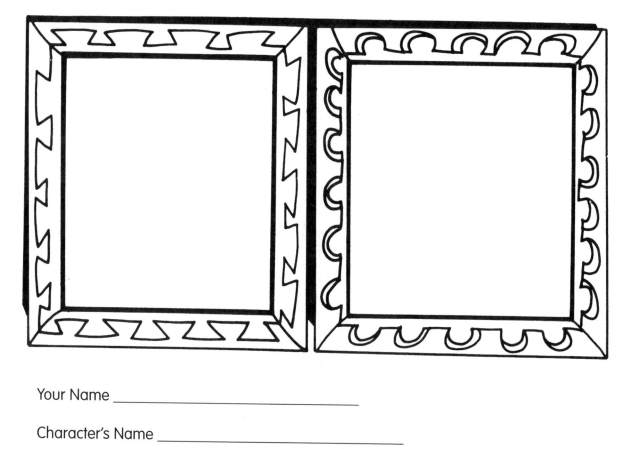

Your Name _____

Character's Name _____

List four things you have in common with this character.

1. _____

2. _____

3. _____

4. _____

The Lost Pages

Materials

- reading selection
- drawing paper
- crayons or markers
- construction paper
- bookbinding materials

Read a short story or book to the class. Ask students to think about what it would be like to be a character in the story. Divide the class into small groups. Have students discuss how they would help the main characters in the story to work on their problem or conflict. Encourage them to talk about how they would relate to the other characters in the story. Which characters would be their friends? Which characters would they want to know more about? Then, give each student a piece of drawing paper. Have students draw themselves in a scene of the story. Use the pages to make a class book. Create a construction paper cover, and title the book *The Lost Pages of* _____. Insert the title of the book or story in the blank, and bind the pages together.

The Lost Pages of Jack and the Beanstalk by Miss Hermich's 2nd grade

Alike and Different

Materials

- Alike and Different reproducible (page 84)
- overhead transparency/ projector
- reading selections

Make a class set of the Alike and Different reproducible, and make an additional copy on an overhead transparency. Read aloud a story that contains more than two characters. Use the Venn diagram on the reproducible to model how you are alike and different from two of the characters in the story. Verbalize your thought process as you record the similarities and differences between yourself and the characters you selected. Use the information from the diagram to complete the sentences at the bottom of the reproducible. Give each student a copy of the reproducible. Have students use two characters from their favorite story to complete the Venn diagram. Have students discuss their diagram as a class. Hang the diagrams on a bulletin board display near your classroom library.

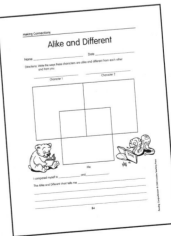

Alike and Different

Name _____   Date _____

Directions: Write the ways these characters are alike and different from each other
and from you.

_____   _____
Character 1   Character 2

Me

I compared myself to _____ and_____.

The Alike and Different chart tells me _____

_____

_____

_____.

Reading Comprehension © 2000 Creative Teaching Press

What's Familiar

Materials

- reading selection
- chart paper

Read aloud a story to students. Ask them to think about what in the story reminds them of something from their own life (e.g., the story is set in a town similar to the one where they live, a character lives in a similar house or apartment building, the characters play games that are familiar). Invite students to make as many connections between their own life and the story as they can. Record these observations on a piece of chart paper titled *What's Familiar.* Try to elicit enough information to fill the entire piece of paper. Then, direct students' attention to the list on the paper. Comment on the great amount of connections they made between what they read and their own lives. Tell students that books become more real when we connect them to our own lives. Encourage them to make these connections when they read independently.

Connections Mural

Materials

- butcher paper
- markers
- container
- age-appropriate novel

In advance, cover a bulletin board or a section of a wall with butcher paper. Leave several markers in a container near the bulletin board display. Select an age-appropriate novel to read aloud to students. Write the title at the top of the butcher paper. Schedule short blocks of time each day to read aloud from the novel. As you read, ask students to pay attention to details in the story that connect to their own lives. Stop periodically during the reading session, and ask students to share their connections. Invite students who make a connection to use a marker to record it on the butcher paper after the reading session. Have students sign their name underneath their writing. Use the display as the focus of a class discussion when you complete the novel. Have students discuss the many ways a story can relate to their lives.

Fairy Tale Rewrites

Materials

- a version of *The Little Red Hen*
- chart paper

Read aloud the story of *The Little Red Hen.* Ask students to relate experiences they have had that are similar to the hen's (e.g., asked someone for help and didn't receive it). Ask students if they have ever been in the position of one of the animals that refused to help the hen (e.g., they told someone no or were too busy to help when asked). Work with students to create a new version of *The Little Red Hen.* Write a story on chart paper, together as a class, with the same theme. Perhaps the story could focus on one student asking others to help build a village from blocks. Everyone is too busy to help build, but once the village is complete, everyone wants to play. After the shared writing experience, divide the class into small groups, and have each group act out the story.

> Too Busy to Build
>
> Rita decided to build a city with blocks. She asked her friend Tom to help her.

Connected Tales

Materials

- Connected Tales reproducible (page 87)
- two versions of the same fairy tale
- overhead transparency/ projector

In advance, find a fairy tale that has many different versions, such as *Cinderella* or *The Three Little Pigs.* Choose two versions of the fairy tale to read aloud to the class. Organize students into small groups of three or four. Make a copy of the Connected Tales reproducible for each group, and make an additional copy on an overhead transparency. Read aloud both versions of the fairy tale. Then, ask each group to discuss how the two stories were alike and different. Have the group members record their observations on the reproducible. Next, invite the groups to share their answers with the rest of the class. Record each group's responses on the transparency. Help students notice that they can make connections between books in the same way they can connect books to their own lives.

Connected Tales

Names _____   _____

_____   _____

Fairy Tale #1   Fairy Tale #2

_____   _____

Write the ways these fairy tales are the same.

_____

_____

_____

_____

Write the ways these fairy tales are different.

_____

_____

_____

_____

Character Buddies

Materials

- chart paper
- glue
- construction paper

Ask students to list all the characters they can remember from stories the class has read. Have them think of characters from read-alouds, shared readings, and stories from your reading program. Record the list of characters on chart paper. Next, ask students to review the list and think about which of the characters had something in common. Spend some time discussing those similarities. Ask students to select two characters from the list, each from a different story, that they think would be friends. Have students write a paragraph explaining why the characters would get along. Glue the papers on colorful construction paper, and post them on a bulletin board display for all to read and enjoy.

> Character List
> Amelia Bedelia   Charlotte
> Arthur   Wilbur
> Francine   Marvin Redpost
> D.W.   Amber Brown
> Mr. Ratburn   Mrs. Piggle-Wiggle
> Muffy

Story-to-Story Connections

Materials

- Story-to-Story Connections reproducible (page 89)

Give each student a copy of the Story-to-Story Connections reproducible. Ask students to think about two stories they have read. Have students record on the reproducible how the two stories were alike and different. Remind them how to use a Venn diagram, and provide an example if needed. Tell students to refer back to the stories if they need additional details to complete the reproducible. Allot time for students to share their Story-to-Story Connections with their classmates.

88

Story-to-Story Connections

Name _____   Date _____

Directions: Compare how two stories that you have read are alike and different.

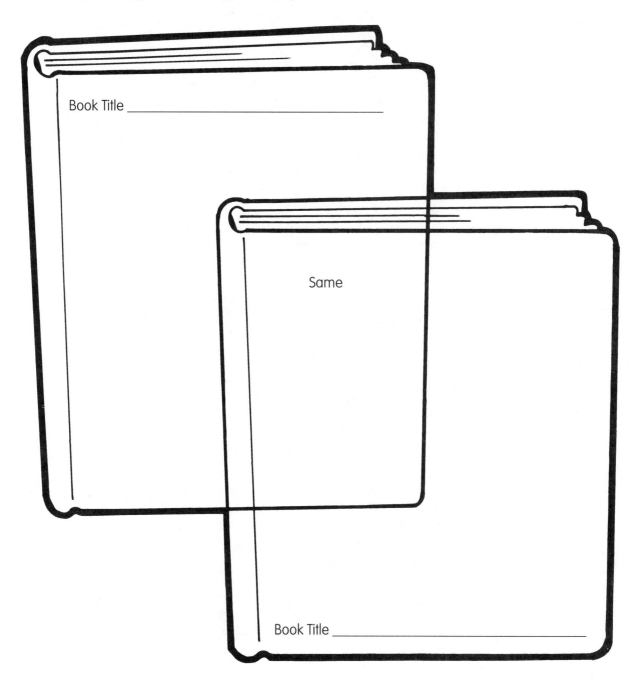

Book Title _____

Same

Book Title _____

Connection Chains

Materials

- Connection Chains reproducibles (pages 91–93)
- copy paper (assorted colors)
- index cards
- tape
- containers
- scissors
- glue

Make many copies of the Connection Chains reproducibles. Copy each of the three reproducibles on a different color of copy paper. Write *Book-to-Myself, Book-to-My-World,* and *Book-to-Book* on separate index cards, and tape each label to a separate container. Cut apart the reproducible chain cards, and sort them into the matching containers placed near your classroom library. Add an additional container for students' completed cards, and label it *Chain.* Introduce each kind of card to students. Have students recall the connections they have made between books and themselves, books and the world around them, and two different books. Invite students to continue thinking about these connections as they read independently. When students make a connection, have them take the appropriate colored card and fill it out. Have students place their completed cards in the container labeled *Chain.* Periodically invite student volunteers to assist you in turning the cards into a chain by linking the cards together and gluing them. (Be sure to glue chains word-side out so you will be able to read them.) Hang the paper chain from the walls or ceiling of your classroom. When it is long enough, attach it from one side of the room to the other. Have students count the colored links to determine which types of connections they make most often.

Book Connections Board

Materials

- butcher paper
- yarn
- colored markers
- stapler

Cover a bulletin board with butcher paper. Divide the paper into three columns. Label the columns *Connections to Myself, Connections to My World,* and *Connections to Other Books.* Attach a different-colored marker to each column by tying one end of the marker to a piece of yarn and stapling the other end of the yarn to the bulletin board. Then, have students think about the three types of connections when they read independently. Have students record their name, the book title, and the author of their book under the appropriate category when they make a connection in one of the three areas. Once a week, have students discuss the connections they made.

Connection Chains

Book-to-Myself

Name _____ Book Title _____

I made a connection between this book and myself.

This book reminds me of _____

_____

Book-to-Myself

Name _____ Book Title _____

I made a connection between this book and myself.

This book reminds me of _____

_____

Book-to-Myself

Name _____ Book Title _____

I made a connection between this book and myself.

This book reminds me of _____

_____

91

Connection Chains

Book-to-My-World

Name _____

_____ Book Title

I made a connection between this book and the world.

This book reminds me of _____

_____

Book-to-My-World

Name _____

_____ Book Title

I made a connection between this book and the world.

This book reminds me of _____

_____

Book-to-My-World

Name _____

_____ Book Title

I made a connection between this book and the world.

This book reminds me of _____

_____

Connection Chains

Book-to-Book

Name _____ Book Title _____

I made a connection between this book and another book I have read.

This book reminds me of _____

_____

Book-to-Book

Name _____ Book Title _____

I made a connection between this book and another book I have read.

This book reminds me of _____

_____

Book-to-Book

Name _____ Book Title _____

I made a connection between this book and another book I have read.

This book reminds me of _____

_____

93

Monitoring Growth

Assessing a student's level of comprehension at the beginning of the school year is important for determining baseline data and planning for instruction. Equally important is the ongoing assessment that takes place throughout the year. Monitoring the individual growth of your students will enable you to meet the needs of students who are having difficulty and challenge those who are developing at an accelerated rate. You will also have a clear idea of how to plan and pace your whole-class and small-group instruction. Keeping an accurate and up-to-date record of your students' achievements will also help you maintain clear communication with parents.

Use the Growth Chart reproducibles (pages 95–96) to record student progress in each of the reading strategies outlined in this book. Copy one chart for each student in your class. Store the growth chart in a file folder or reading portfolio for each student, or keep all the charts in a three-ring binder. The following suggestions provide different methods for using the growth chart as an assessment tool to monitor progress in reading comprehension:

- Meet with each student individually once each grading period. Have the student read a short selection, and record anecdotal notes on the growth chart as you observe the student's use of each strategy. Discuss the story with the student to assess his or her understanding of specific strategies listed on the chart.
- Teach each strategy individually. Record on each chart the date you focused on the particular strategy. Then, record the date that you first notice each student applying that strategy. Include any anecdotal information that will help you make judgments about future instructional decisions.
- Remember to assess each student's ability to apply reading strategies outside of the reading group. Record on the chart anecdotal information about a student's reading comprehension in other curricular areas. Note each student's ability to apply reading strategies while working in centers, experimenting with science projects, and reading social studies text.

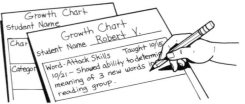

Growth Chart

Student Name _____

Word-Attack Skills

Phrasing and Fluency

Sequencing

Retelling

Predicting

Accessing Prior Knowledge

Growth Chart

Student Name _____

Characterization
Categorization
Identifying the Main Idea
Making Inferences
Making Connections

Reading Comprehension © 2000 Creative Teaching Press